Disney's

## THE LITTLE MERMAID

# An Under the Sea
# CHRISTMAS

### A Holiday Songbook

*A Musical Note*

Sebastian, King Triton's royal court composer, is from the Caribbean Sea, where they like to play their Christmas carols—and everything else, for that matter—with a special island beat. Sometimes it's a smooth calypso pulse, sometimes a wild reggae rhythm. You may want to try playing the Christmas carols in this book the way Sebastian and the Crustacean Band might perform them—with a Caribbean flavor. You can do this by creating your own Caribbean percussion section. If you have a tambourine, a bongo drum, a maraca or two—use them. If not, a metal pan makes a good steel drum, and a wooden spoon is a perfect drumstick. Just round up as many instruments and amateur percussionists as you want, and play along as you sing!

FIRST EDITION
1 3 5 7 9 10 8 6 4 2

Library of Congress Catalog Card Number: 93-70939
ISBN: 1-56282-504-6

Musical arrangements by Steve Aprahamian

# Contents

IT WAS CHRISTMAS MORNING UNDER THE SEA, and King Triton's seven daughters—Ariel, Adella, Alana, Andrina, Aquata, Arista, and Attina— were all gathered in the palace music room. Sebastian, the royal court composer and conductor, was trying to get the princesses to rehearse the Christmas carols they would be performing that evening.

"Girls, girls!" he cried, rapping his baton on his music stand. "We must begin. This is our last rehearsal before the royal holiday celebration."

Usually Ariel and her sisters worked very hard at their music lessons and during rehearsals. They all had beautiful voices and loved to sing. But today they were far too excited to pay attention—there were just too many other things to think about.

"What are you going to wear to the party tonight?" Adella asked Ariel. "I want to go out to the oyster beds to find some new pearls for my hair."

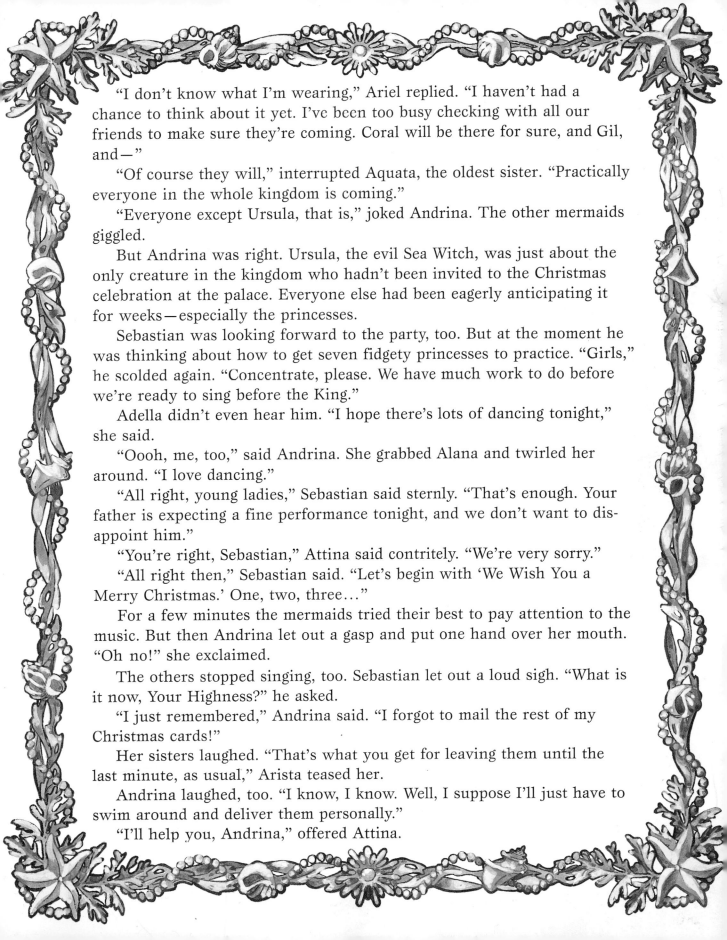

"I don't know what I'm wearing," Ariel replied. "I haven't had a chance to think about it yet. I've been too busy checking with all our friends to make sure they're coming. Coral will be there for sure, and Gil, and—"

"Of course they will," interrupted Aquata, the oldest sister. "Practically everyone in the whole kingdom is coming."

"Everyone except Ursula, that is," joked Andrina. The other mermaids giggled.

But Andrina was right. Ursula, the evil Sea Witch, was just about the only creature in the kingdom who hadn't been invited to the Christmas celebration at the palace. Everyone else had been eagerly anticipating it for weeks—especially the princesses.

Sebastian was looking forward to the party, too. But at the moment he was thinking about how to get seven fidgety princesses to practice. "Girls," he scolded again. "Concentrate, please. We have much work to do before we're ready to sing before the King."

Adella didn't even hear him. "I hope there's lots of dancing tonight," she said.

"Oooh, me, too," said Andrina. She grabbed Alana and twirled her around. "I love dancing."

"All right, young ladies," Sebastian said sternly. "That's enough. Your father is expecting a fine performance tonight, and we don't want to disappoint him."

"You're right, Sebastian," Attina said contritely. "We're very sorry."

"All right then," Sebastian said. "Let's begin with 'We Wish You a Merry Christmas.' One, two, three…"

For a few minutes the mermaids tried their best to pay attention to the music. But then Andrina let out a gasp and put one hand over her mouth. "Oh no!" she exclaimed.

The others stopped singing, too. Sebastian let out a loud sigh. "What is it now, Your Highness?" he asked.

"I just remembered," Andrina said. "I forgot to mail the rest of my Christmas cards!"

Her sisters laughed. "That's what you get for leaving them until the last minute, as usual," Arista teased her.

Andrina laughed, too. "I know, I know. Well, I suppose I'll just have to swim around and deliver them personally."

"I'll help you, Andrina," offered Attina.

Sebastian rapped his baton again, more sharply this time. "You may all deliver whatever you like to whomever you like—*after* the rehearsal is over," he said.

"Sorry, Sebastian," the mermaids said in unison. Again they settled down and began to practice.

A few minutes later Attina couldn't help leaning over to ask Alana a question. "Do you think I'll get many books this year?" she whispered.

Alana burst out laughing. "You'll probably *only* get books again, Attina, just like last year. The whole ocean knows they're your favorite gift!"

"Girls!" Sebastian scolded. "Please! I must insist that you be quiet! Otherwise we won't be finished until dinnertime!"

"Dinner!" Adella said eagerly. "I can't wait to see what delicious things Cook comes up with this year. Do you remember those seaweed biscuits he served last Christmas?" She licked her lips hungrily.

Sebastian let out another long, deep sigh. "I give up," he said, waving his claws. "Why don't you girls just get all your talking and planning done first, and then perhaps we can continue without further interruption." He turned away with a frown.

At that, the mermaids all began chattering at once.

"Let's all go out on a sleigh ride later," Arista said excitedly. "I have some bells I can put on Foamy and the other sea horses so they'll jingle."

"It will be such fun to decorate the Great Concert Hall for the party," Ariel said dreamily, remembering the spectacular decorations they'd had the year before.

"Oh, yes!" said Attina. "I can't wait to help trim the tree. Alana and I spent all last week gathering starfish for it. It's going to be beautiful."

"Well, don't forget, I found the pearls for the tree," Adella said.

"Yes, Adella, and weren't you also the one who found the sea mistletoe?" Alana reminded her.

Adella blushed. She hadn't wanted her sisters to know that she was the one who'd hung a piece of sea mistletoe above the ballroom door, since she was afraid they'd guess she was hoping to kiss a very special merboy under it. But with six sisters, it was hard to keep a secret!

"I'm also really looking forward to singing Christmas carols," Ariel said. "The songs Sebastian picked out are…Oh! Sebastian!" She looked over at the crab, who was now watching them with his claws crossed over his chest.

The sisters exchanged glances. "At this rate we'll never stop talking in time to practice," Arista said quietly.

The others nodded. "We're sorry, Sebastian," Aquata said. "You've been very patient."

"It's just that there's so much to think about," Attina explained. "After all, it *is* Christmas."

Ariel glanced at her sisters. "I know something that might help make it up to Sebastian," she told them. "Let's give him his Christmas present early!"

"Hmph," Sebastian said. He still looked annoyed, but he also looked curious. "You girls are just trying to distract me so I won't make you rehearse, aren't you?"

"No, no, Sebastian," Ariel assured him sincerely. "I just think this present will show you how much we really do appreciate you, even if we don't always show it."

"Ariel's right," Aquata added. "Please say you'll open it now—it will take only a second."

Sebastian hesitated, but finally his curiosity got the better of him. He couldn't wait to find out what the princesses were giving him for Christmas. "All right then, I'll open it if it will make you happy. But hurry," he said, trying to sound stern.

Attina rushed off to get the gift. A moment later she returned carrying a beautifully wrapped package. It was long and thin and was tied with a big bow.

"For me?" Sebastian said, taking the gift. "What is it?"

"Open it!" Ariel urged.

Sebastian carefully unwrapped the package. When he saw what was inside, he gasped. "It's beautiful!" he exclaimed, pulling out the sparkling crystal conductor's baton. "Thank you, girls! How did you know?"

The mermaids exchanged smiles. "I guess we just know you pretty well, Sebastian," Ariel answered for all of them.

Sebastian put aside the old baton he'd been using and held up the new one. "Then you probably know that there's one more Christmas gift you girls could give me that would make me the happiest crab in the sea," he said.

The princesses looked at one another, puzzled. "What's that, Sebastian?" asked Aquata.

He smiled. "You could settle down and finish your rehearsal!"

The mermaids all laughed. And then they did just as he asked.

# We Wish You a Merry Christmas

*Happily*

*Traditional English*

# Deck the Halls

# Christmas Is Coming

# Jolly Old Saint Nicholas

# O Christmas Tree

# O Come, All Ye Faithful

Translated by Rev. F. Oakeley
*Latin Hymn*

# The Holly and the Ivy

*Andante*

*Traditional French Melody*

The hol-ly and— the i-vy, now both— are full— well grown,— of all the trees with-in the woods, the hol-ly bears the crown.— O the ris-ing of the sun, the run-ning of— the deer,— the play-ing of the merry or-gan, sweet sing-ing in— the choir,— sweet sing-ing in the choir.—

# Away in a Manger

# Jingle Bells

**Brightly**

James Pierpont

mf Dash - ing through the snow, in a one-horse o - pen sleigh;

o'er the fields we go, laugh-ing all the way;

*(continued on page 28)*

28

# I Saw Three Ships

# The First Noel

# Joy to the World

Words by Isaac Watts
Music by G. F. Handel

*Joyfully*

**ff**

1. Joy to the world! The Lord is come; let earth re-
2. Joy to the world! The Sav - ior reigns; let men their
3. He rules the world with truth and grace, and makes the

ceive her King; Let ev - 'ry heart pre -
songs em - ploy; while fields and floods, rocks,
na - tions prove the glo - ries of His

pare Him room, and heav'n and na - ture sing, and heav'n and na - ture
hills, and plains re - peat the sound-ing joy, re - peat the sound-ing
righ - teous - ness and won - ders of His love, and won - ders of His

sing, and heav'n and heav'n and na - ture sing.
joy, re - peat re - peat and the sound - ing joy.
love, and won - ders and won - ders of his love.

# Hark! The Herald Angels Sing

Words by Charles Wesley
Music by Felix Mendelssohn

(continued on page 38)

36

# O Come, Little Children

*Words by Christoph von Schmid*
*Traditional German*

# Silent Night

Words by Joseph Mohr
Music by Franz Gruber

# It Came Upon the Midnight Clear

*Words by Edmund H. Sears*
*Music by R. S. Willis*

# Auld Lang Syne

Words by Robert Burns
Traditional Scottish

*Melancholy*

*p* Should old ac-quaint-ance be for-got, and___ nev-er brought to mind? Should old ac-quaint-ance be for-got, and___ days of auld lang syne? For

46